the art of Gulammohammed Sheikh

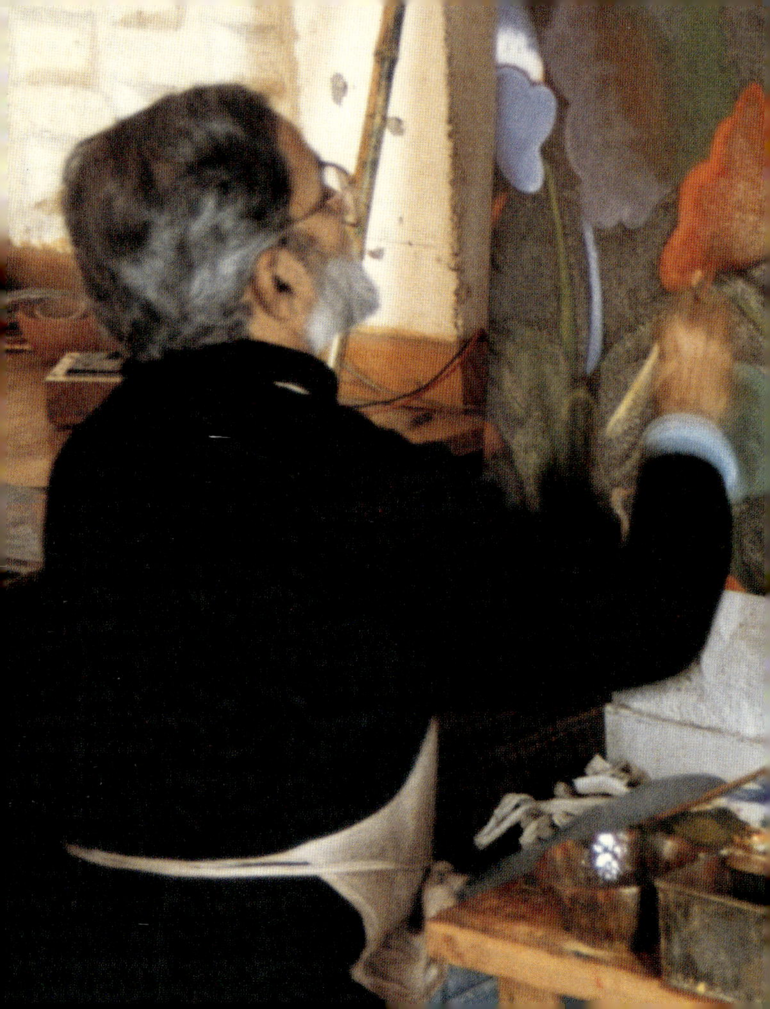

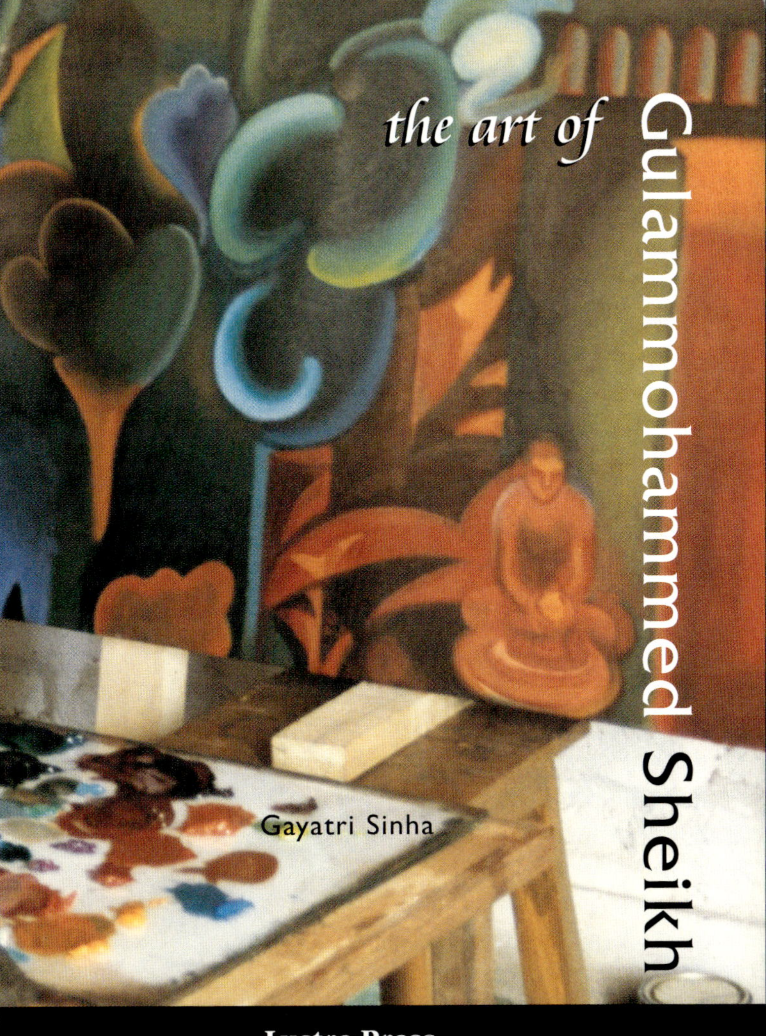

the art of Gulammohammed Sheikh

Gayatri Sinha

Lustre Press
Roli Books

Imagine the eye as a periscope that miniaturises the most wayward detail; imagine the mind of a fabulist who recreates the stuff of boyhood dreams, and enlist the scholar who compresses and weaves together the pages of art history: Gulammohammed Sheikh challenges his viewer with such a slew of visual material. On a canvas imploding with detail, Sheikh is critically observant of Indian public life, while maintaining a lilting romantic affinity to his own vision.

Gulam Sheikh's painting, particularly of the last two decades, seeks to question and resolve. Born in 1937 in the small town of Surendranagar in Kathiawar, Gujarat, the *mohalla* in which he grew up left decisive memories such as an impenetrable wall, that stretched from the river bed to the crowded town beyond. It appears in paintings like *The Wall* and *Beyond the Wall.* The Gaekwadi maidan behind his home, the dried bed of the river Bhogavo and the slaughterhouse next door defined his first memories of space and enclosure. His father – a devout Muslim, his mother, who cooked endless meals in a darkened room over the cowdung fire, the *faqirkhana* nearby are recalled with the same searing intensity as are stories of *jinns* and ghouls and mythical forms. 'As a little boy I would sit in a half-darkened room to draw pictures . . . Seated by the lantern at night, watching our shadows grow and dip with the wavering flame, I felt a *jinnaat* sitting next to me.'

Gulammohammed completed his M.A. in painting in 1961 from the MS University, Baroda. By this time he had already been recognised as a writer of promise. In 1962 he

Working on a gouache in Mumbai

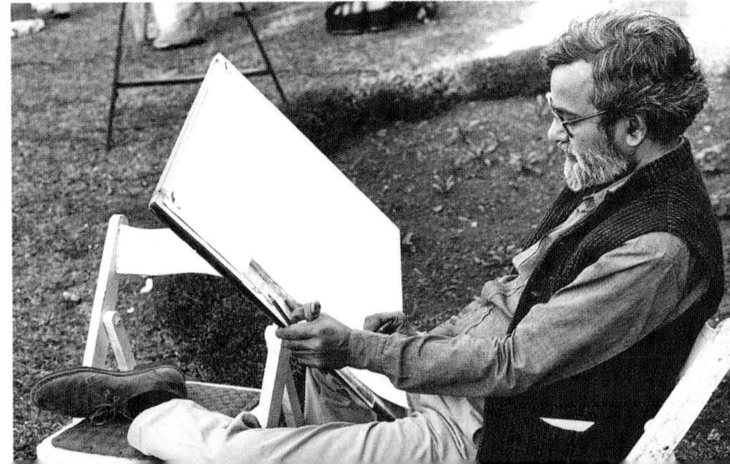

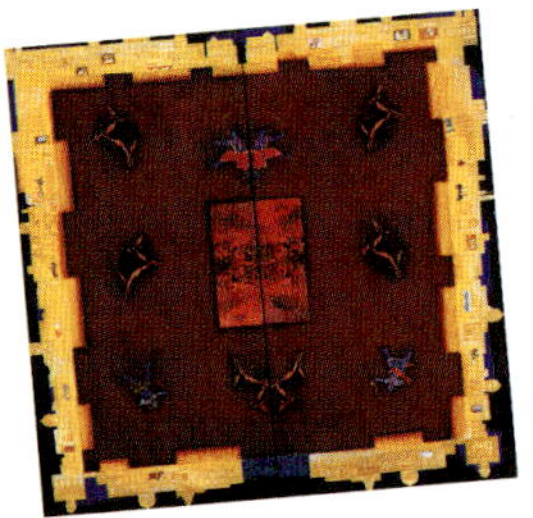
Mirage

won the National Award for *The Chase* and participated in the Tokyo biennale in 1963. In the same year, he became a founder-member of the seminal Group 1890, with J. Swaminathan and other artists. The group's only collective exhibition vigorously articulated the need for an Indian modernism, a position that Sheikh has maintained and further refined. During these formative years, he made semi-abstract works in a thick impasto. From 1963 to 1966 he studied at the Royal College of Art in London, when the abstraction and pop movement were beginning to peter out. He regularly visited the abundant collection of Indian miniature paintings at the Victoria and Albert museum.

Central to the museum's prized collection are the Hamza Nama paintings, commissioned by the boy-emperor Akbar. Sheikh was struck by the manner in which the paintings had to be scanned like a scroll that is gradually unfurled, rather than viewed with the Western definition of perspective. The illustration of Amir Hamza's romance also struck him for its proximity to a real state in which violence and an intense physicality were strongly portrayed. This exposure evoked an answering chord in the artist when he returned home to Kathiawar. 'Returning to my provincial home town I found the layers of time past, which I had seen in paintings, still present, in one form or another; images which were beautiful, serene and deeply moving; images which were disturbing.'

Sheikh began a series of semi-autobiographical essays invoking childhood memories, reinscribing them with the passage of time and experience. The idea of 'home' in which memory and desire collide was central to this series. His seminal work *Returning Home After a Long Absence* (1969-73) derives from a keen sense of the fabulous and the quotidian, and marked this shift in sensibility. In the right corner angels alight on trees, while the buraq bearing its heavenly visitant, the Prophet, rides across the skies. Marked out by a wall stand a cluster of houses, oddly unpeopled and still, while in the foreground, virtually advancing out of the frame, is the artist's mother. Her elderly widowed figure, cut in half by the frame carries a presentiment of the issues of life and death. Using elements from Mughal and Persian sources, *Returning Home After a Long Absence* was the first of Sheikh's works about Kathiawar.

During his stay in England and thereafter, Sheikh travelled widely. Early Renaissance Italian art, particularly that of Ambrogio Lorenzetti, inspired him. Lorenzetti's *The Allegory of Good Government* (1338-9) sets a moral tone, portrays an appreciation of architectural elements, and a comprehension of panorama that found an echo in Sheikh's works.

On his return from England Sheikh extended his interest in print- making, participated in the Paris biennale and, in 1969, launched *Vrishchik*, an art magazine, jointly edited with Bhupen Khakhar. The magazine afforded a platform for artists to discuss critical issues, and established

Sheikh's position as an important artist and ideologue.

In the early 1970s Sheikh painted luminous landscapes of pure forms in a heightened palette. Typically Sheikh uses colour to convey sensation. In *Tree Over Mountains* (1970), he used a bright yellow, which lends the work its numinous quality, highlighting the influence of Indian miniatures, or the influence of Henri Rousseau in its quality of suspended animation.

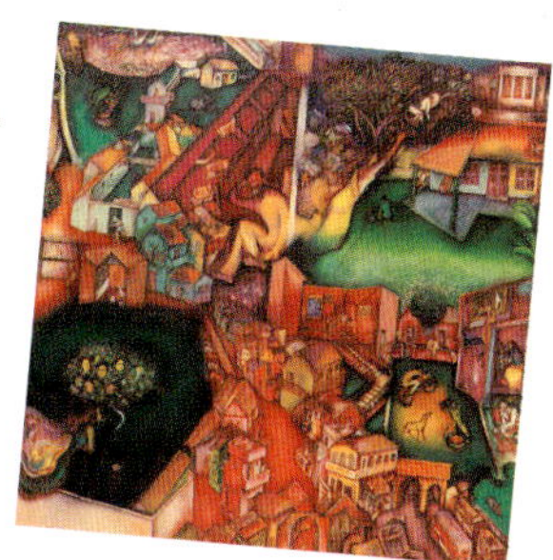

Revolving Routes

In the 1970s, *Speechless City* (1975), a direct response to the emergency and the withdrawal of democratic rights, made waves. One city appears above another; the one below is bereft of human presence but crowded with dogs, crows, and other ominous symbols of absence or death. In *About Waiting and Wandering* and *Revolving Routes,* the multiple points of entry and exit create a plurality of perspective, and possibility of open-ended interpretation. The city remains a central motif, but Sheikh invites us to look into the interiors of homes and courtyards, to recognise attitudes of anticipation and frozen desire. The venality, loneliness, and corruption of the city street, only hinted at in *Speaking Street*, becomes fully blown in his large work *City for Sale* (1981-84). In a way this work epitomises what Sheikh describes as 'my journey through art towards life'. *City for Sale* is a strong critique of communal rioting in India. Located in Baroda, the brutalisation of street life and the chaos that it generates, is ironically offset by the mass pleasure in the escapist Hindi film. The painting compels the viewer as an active

With colleagues and students, Faculty of Fine Arts, Baroda

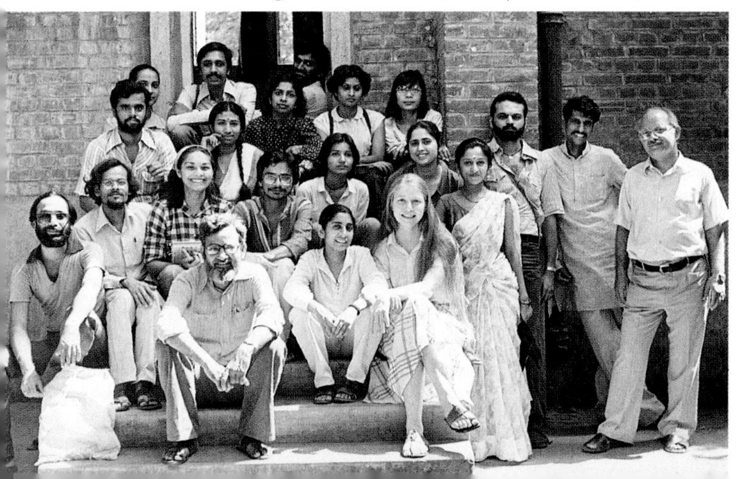

participant to move across its complex surface, which seems to teeter on the brink of a dangerous synapse. The inversion in the scale of values is telling – on the right fore corner stands a miniaturised city; on the left, a cart bearing fruit and vegetables seems to tip into the edge of the frame. The overcrowded human forms that collide with one another speak of the overt conflict of urban Indian experience. The paintings that plot the graph of Gulam's return from England to his critique of public life were exhibited in his solo show titled *Returning Home* at the Centre Georges Pompidou in Paris, in 1985.

As Sheikh's oeuvre developed, two distinct aspects emerged: a vivid palette in which colour rose like a haze or a corpuscular cloud, or even as an emotional determinant through which viewers could 'feel' the painting; the other aspect was his use of architectural devices — walls, enclosures, roof tops, windows, stairways, pillars, which serve as frames to contain and divide multiple narratives (reminiscent of the manner in which space is used in the panels of Bharhut or Amravati) . . . Within each frame, a moment in time is frozen, but through a complex arrangement of interrelationships, these appear to churn and seethe with suppressed energy. The city itself with its tight, spilling structures stands in contrast to nature with its lush plants, thrusting and green with the sap of life. This interest in architecture as a lietmotif finds an echo in his *Jaisalmer* poems (1963) or *Delhi* (1973), in which the city's architectural remnants are invested with a strong emotional quality. Acknowledging the centrality of the city to the contemporary Indian experience, his work portrays the reality of relentless Indian migration and the tension that disparate unplanned growth unleashes.

In the 1980s especially, Sheikh appeared to be preoccupied with the tenor of a society in a state of flux. His paintings are annotations of his leading concerns, his acknowledgement of both the grandeur and debasement in the human situation.

In the same context, Sheikh frequently uses the image of the tree. In *The Wall* or *Returning Home,* the tree becomes the site with transcendental possibilities in which angels alight or other worldly forms live like silent interlocuters with another level of awareness. Associations are evoked with the wish-fulfilling tree or the *Kalpavriksha,* and reference to the *pipal* and *aakda* of his childhood courtyard. In *Meghdoot,* the tree provides cover for nocturnal spirits who watch over middle-class localities and the humdrum activities of daily life. In *Conjurers,* the tree is multi-hued like a bejewelled fountain of desire. And at an apogee, in his large mural for Vidhan Bhavan in Bhopal, titled *Tree of Life,* the tree scape like a cloud burst, is in a sense, Sheikh's own allegory for good government. The civilisational inheritance of Madhya Pradesh, its myths and rich history in the upper reaches of the tree-mural gradually descend into compelling contemporary issues: peoples' representatives, and human and ecological threats like the Union Carbide disaster. Both in terms of its scale and its poetic endeavour, the mural is a marvel of conceptualisation.

More recently there have been subtle shifts in the artist's oeuvre from a formal to a philosophical level. Sheikh has long been an admirer of Kabir as a poet and an iconoclastic Indian figure who absorbs within himself notions of subcontinental religious difference. The corruption of the Indian streetside figure, pronounced in his 1980s' works, becomes transformed with the figure of Kabir, who erases and absorbs the notion of the 'other'. And in this amalgam, the phantasms of the artist's boyhood – the angels and the *jinnaat*, the tangible fears and intangible desires find their resting place, a gentle apotheosis.

Gulam Sheikh has presented Kabir through two exhibitions: Kahat Kabir (1998) and Palimpsest (2001). In the first Kabir is witness to an India driven by the notion of the sacred versus the secular, a post- Pokharan India. In *Palimpsest*, Sheikh, the painter and the writer, creates rich metaphoric and symbolic associations through the conflation of word and image, traditional and modern painting, and notions of the sacred and the secular when posited together.

In fact, here, Sheikh makes a further break with his own style. He creates Kabir as a body fabric in which, as in traditional Indian painting, multiple images within a single frame are invoked. In *Ek Achambha Dekha Re Bhai,* the face of Kabir becomes a proto landscape, in which monks and angels, yogis and bodhisattvas, the prophet and pilgrims traverse in a historical quest, even as odd inversions take place: a lion enters a cow's frame, a missile contains a man's body . . . The work has an oddly timeless quality, of a spiritual quest across the vast Eurasian land mass and the inversions of human nature which are common to all times. Perhaps the single work in which his language of painting and social concerns meld the most is *Mirage* (2001). The central image is of the Indian temple town, notably the *ghats* of Ayodhya. Within its highly defined architecture he places delicately miniaturised figures of deer being chased by Rama, completely reminiscent of the gentle idylls of Pahari painting. But with this apparent sport of chasing the elusive golden deer, the painter has used a photographic image of the actual demolition of the Babri Masjid. Closer enquiry reveals that the gilded interiors of the temple town are full of crass objects of desire – Maruti cars, Amitabh Bachchan on television, Ramanand Sagar's Ramayana – and the critique of contemporary India is complete.

While identifying himself firmly as a commentator of our times, Sheikh draws on world art, literature, and popular culture to craft a language that is true to India's civilisational inheritance – her own peculiar modernity. The scale of his references is vast; the possibilities that they open for future painters are innumerable. For within the corpus of his work, the modern and the Indian, in the fullest sense of the words, are not a contradiction, but a complement.

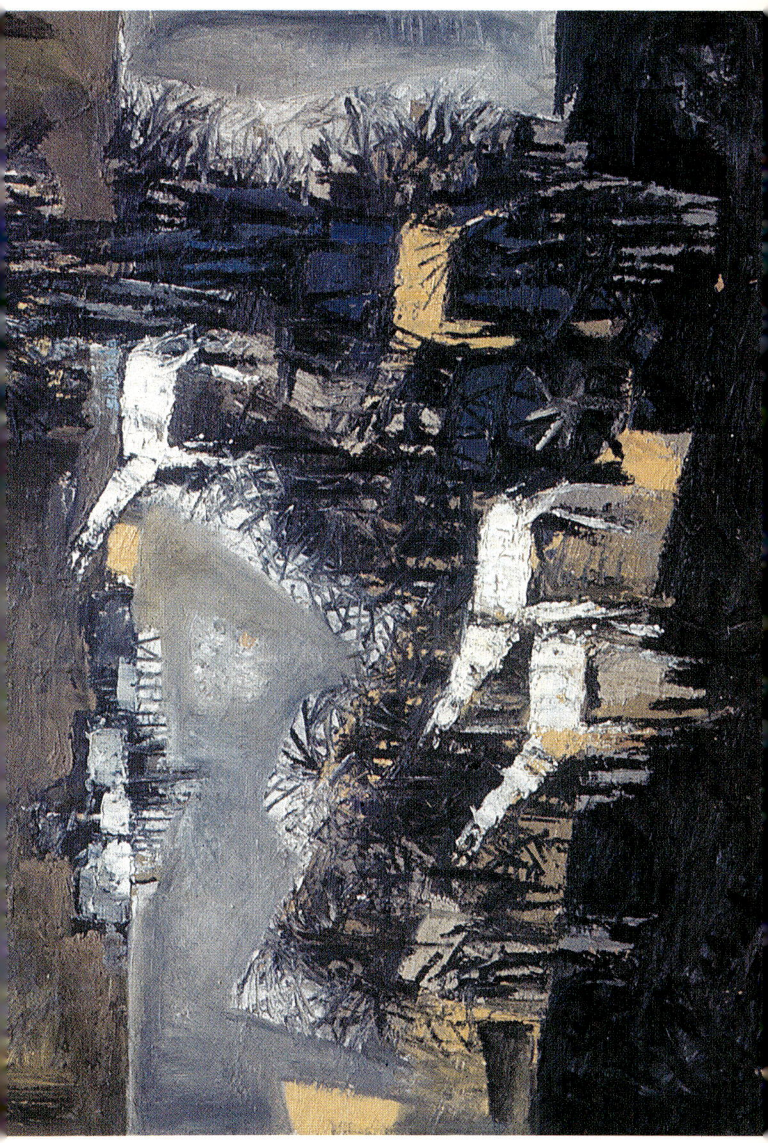

■ Chase

Part of a series of paintings based on the theme of horses. 90 x 121 cm, wax and enamel on hard board, 1961, collection: Mrs Dayal, New Delhi

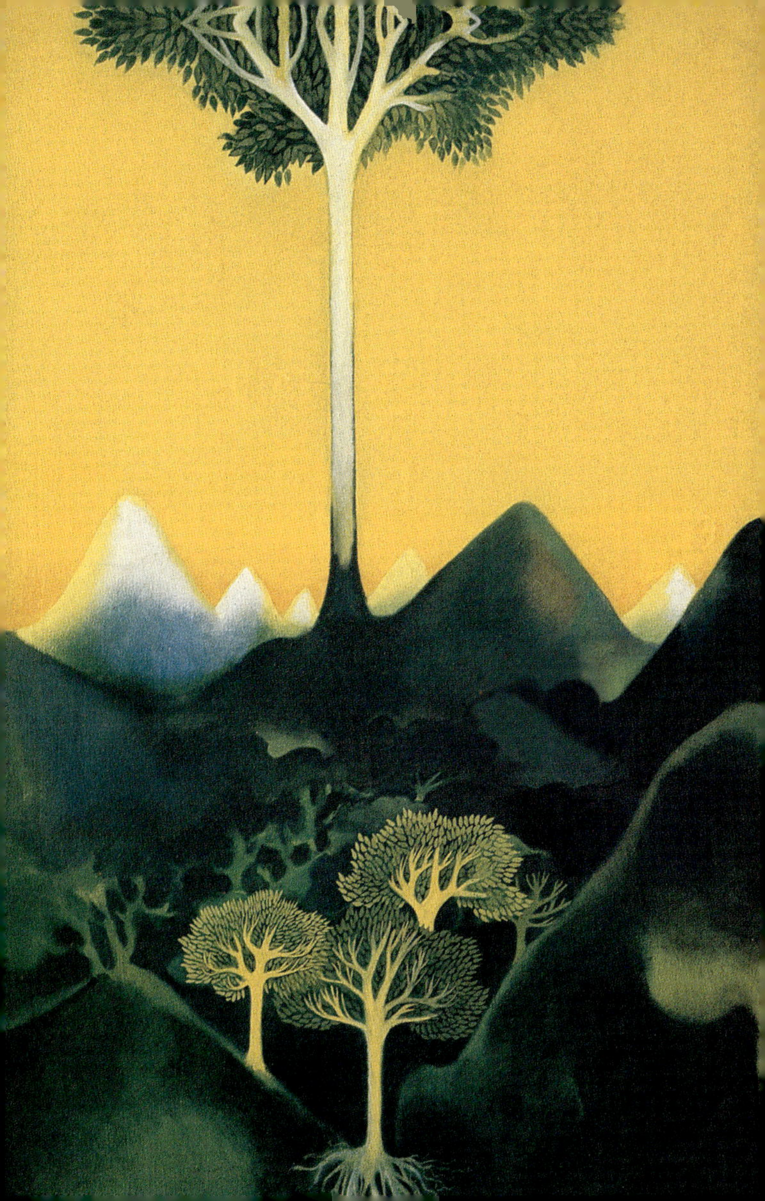

■ Tree over Mountains

Part of a series in which the tree serves as a motif of miraculous presence. 91.5 x 61 cm, oil on canvas, 1970, collection: Aman Nath, New Delhi

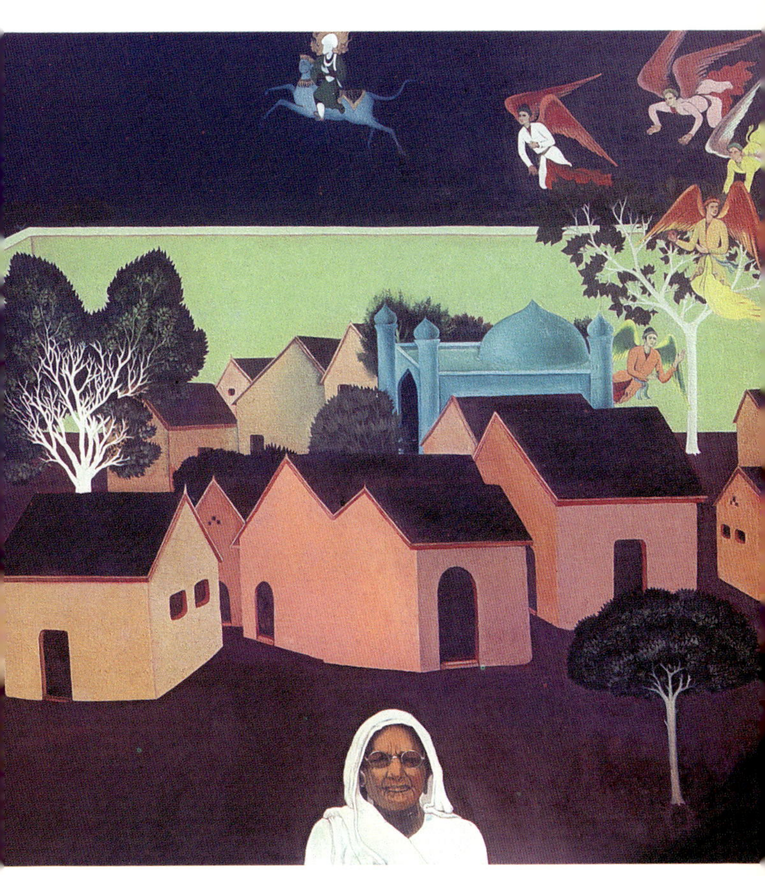

■ Returning Home after a Long Absence

A combination of 'quotes' from a Persian painting, a photograph of the artist's mother and other conjurings.
107 x 107 cm, oil on canvas, 1969-73, collection: Ram and Bharati Sharma

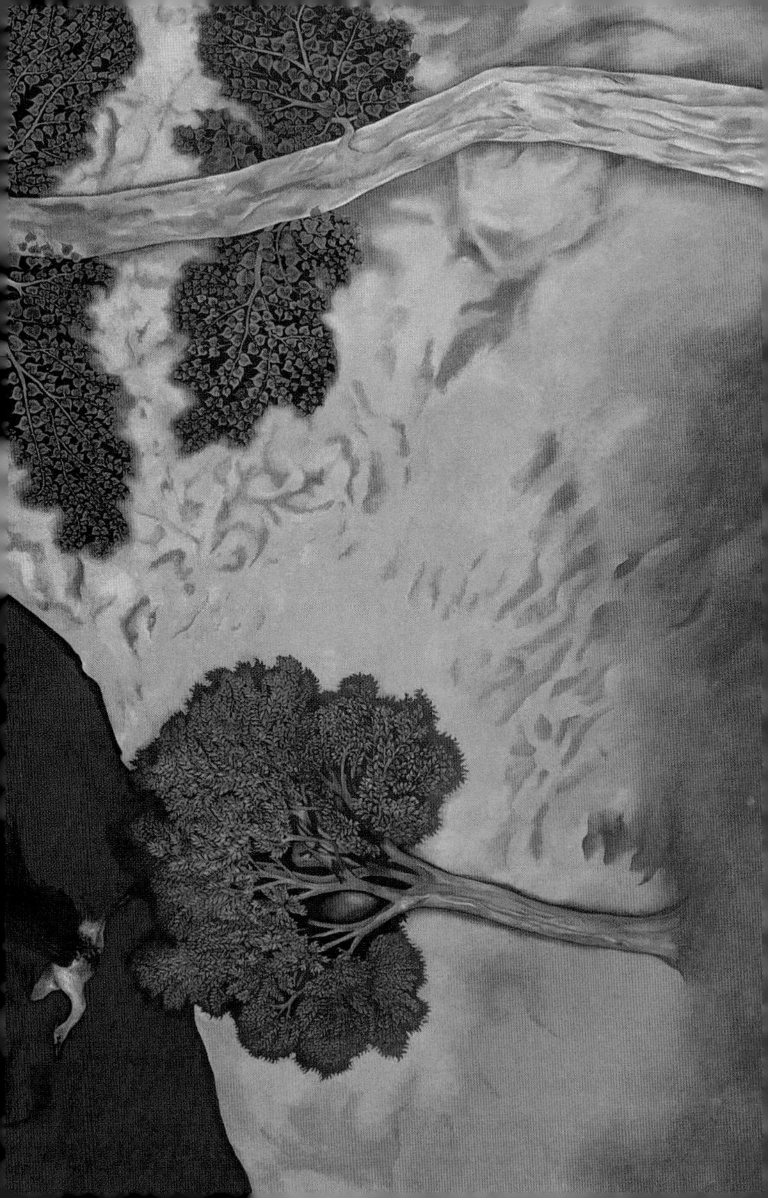

■ Beyond the Trees

Part of a series of paintings that use yellow to evoke a thermal sense of colour. 169.1 x 241.7 cm, oil on canvas, 1977-78, collection: L&T Limited, Mumbai

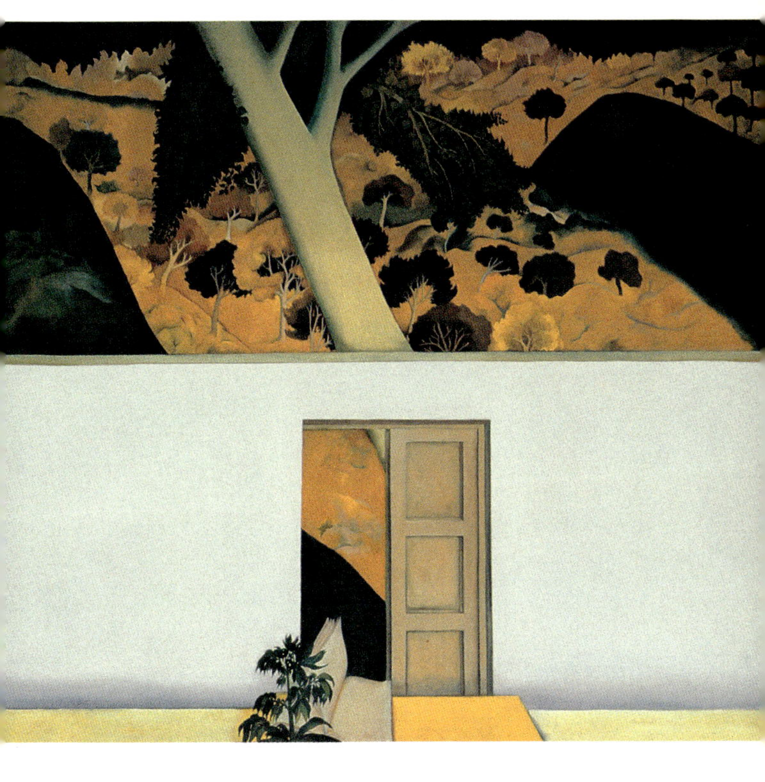

■ The Wall

Worlds on both sides of the wall. 122 x 137.5 cm, oil on canvas, 1976, collection: NGMA (National Gallery of Modern Art), New Delhi

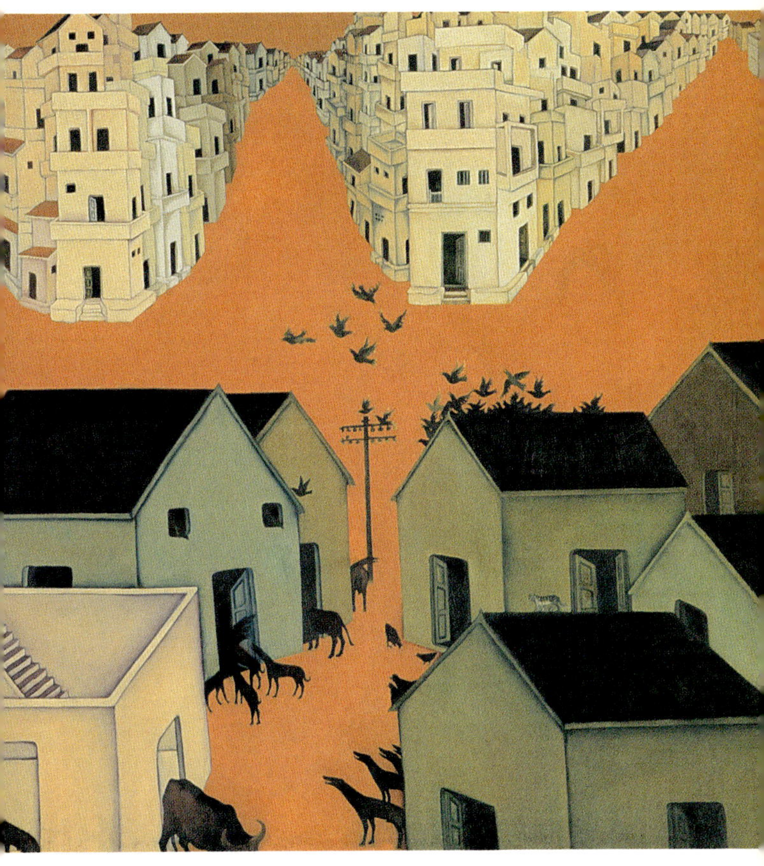

■ Speechless City

Painted during the Emergency: conspicuous absence of human imagery. 107 x 107.2 cm, oil on canvas, 1975, collection: Francis Wacziarg, New Delhi

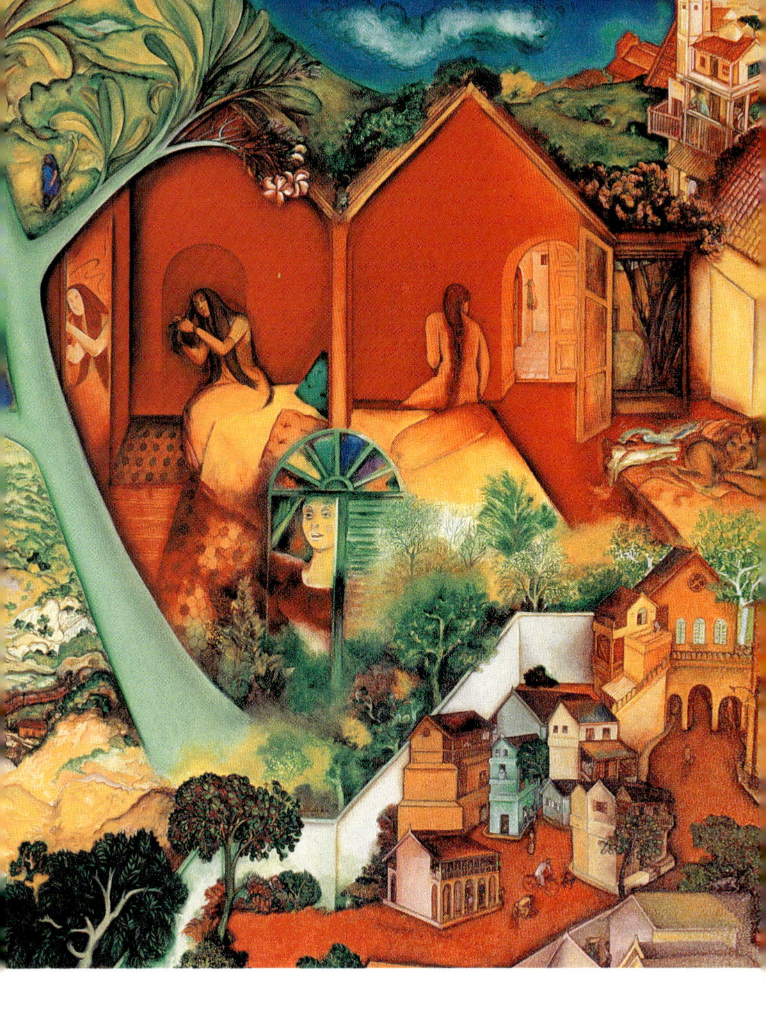

■ About Waiting and Wandering

First in a series of paintings exploring multiple time frames and situations. 137.6 x 114.7 cm, oil on canvas, 1981, collection: Nilima Sheikh, Baroda

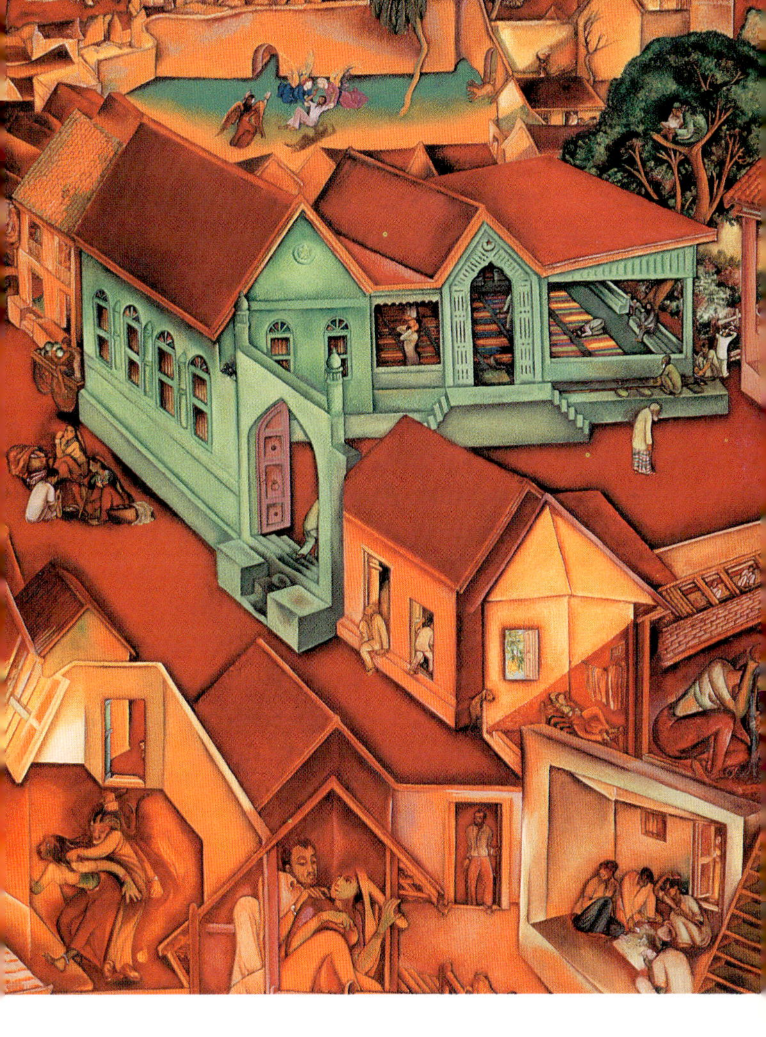

A street scene with a mosque in a mofussil town. 122.7 x 103 cm, oil on canvas, 1981, collection: Roopankar Museum of Fine Arts, Bhopal

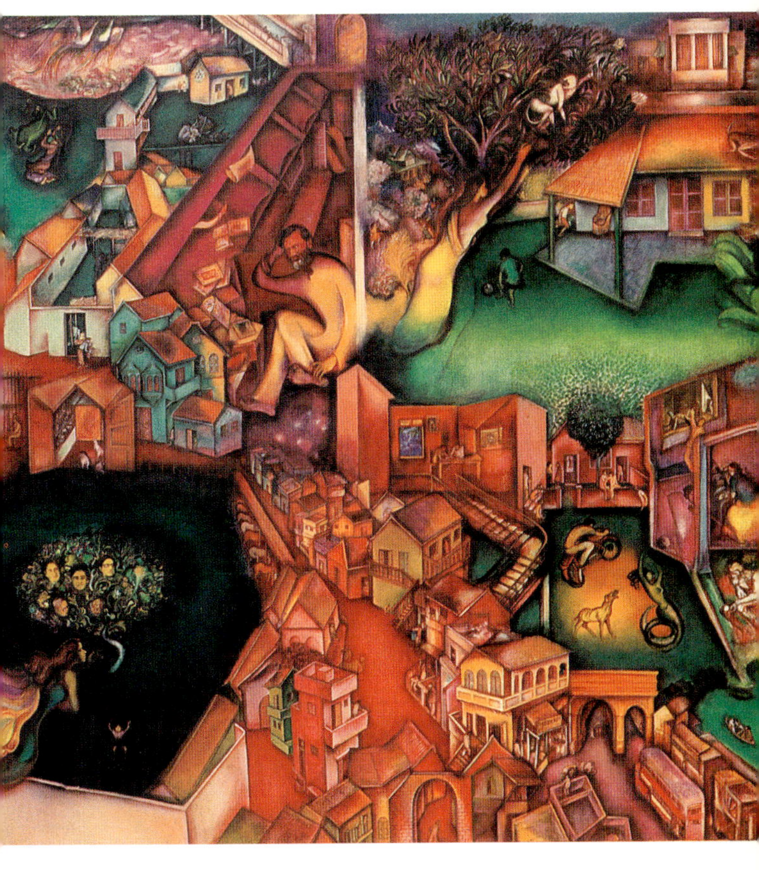

■ Revolving Routes

Multiple situations including a 'Speaking Tree' depicting faces of the artist's friends and mentors. 188 x 188 cm, oil on canvas, 1981, collection: Roopankar Museum of Fine Arts, Bhopal

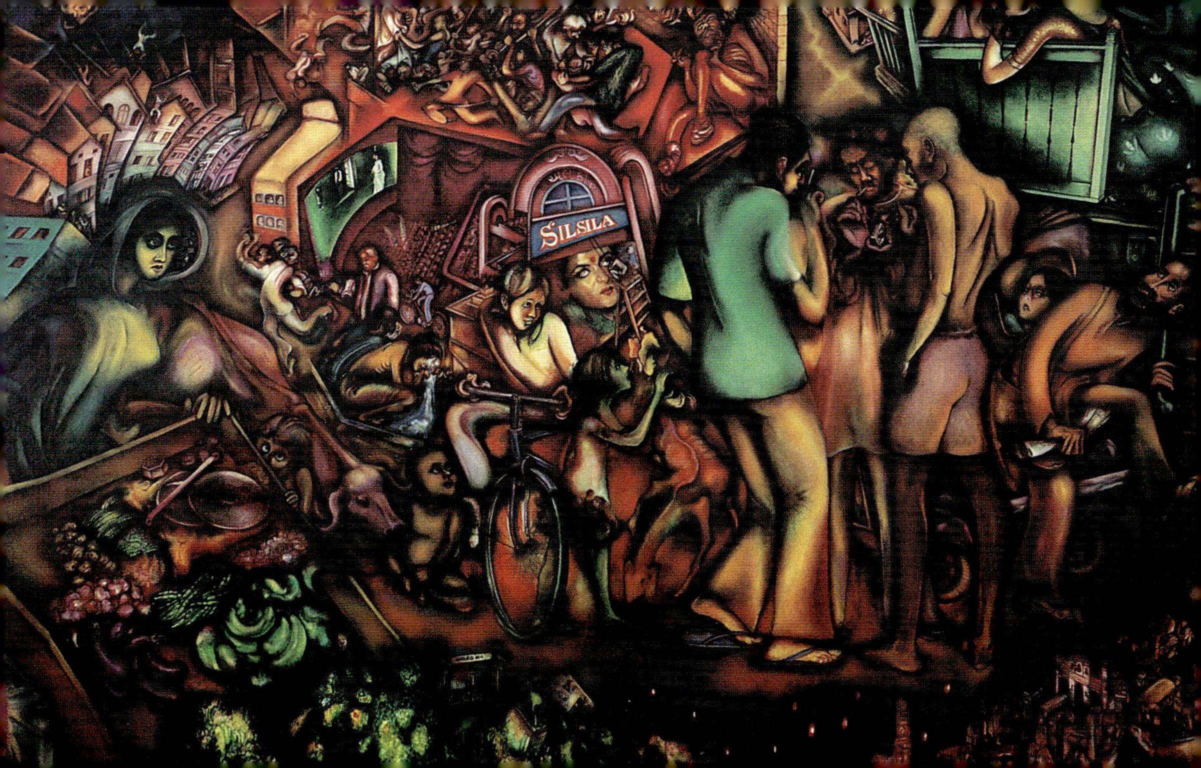

SILSILA

■ City for Sale

A cityscape in the times of communal riots. 223.5 x 305.2 cm, oil on canvas, 1981-84, collection: Trustees of the Victoria and Albert Museum, London

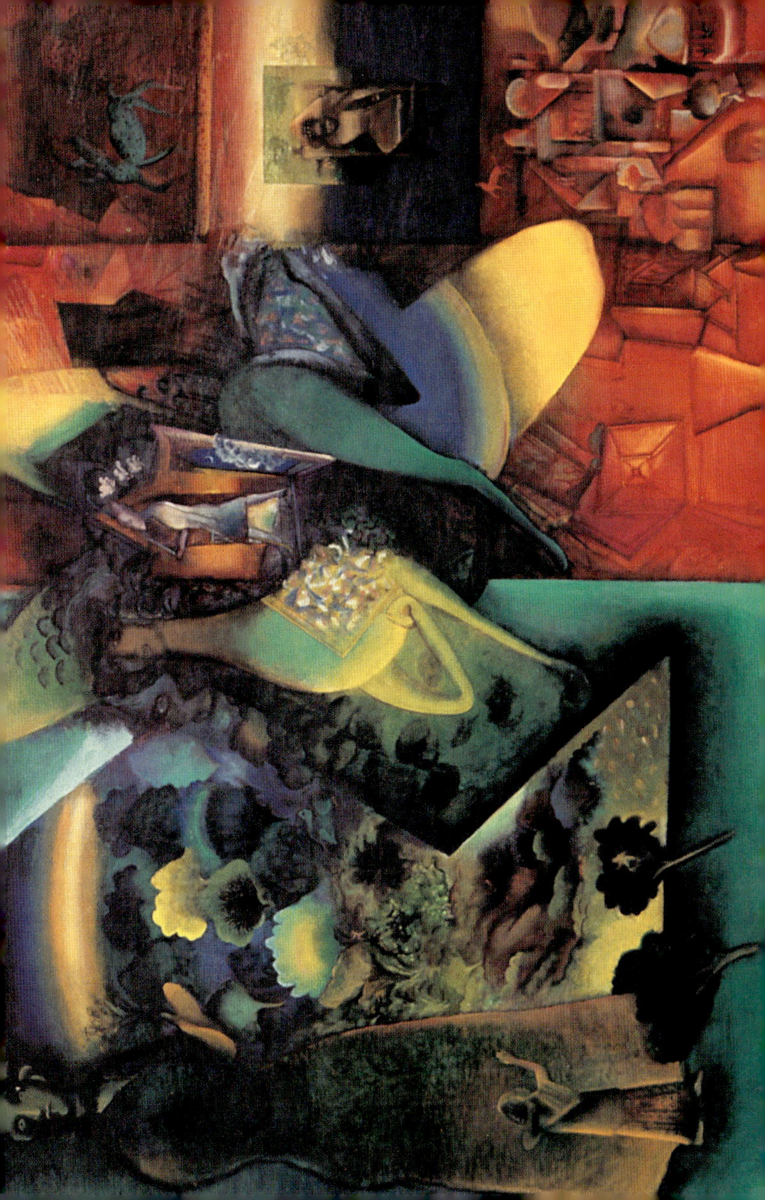

■ Characters Questioning the Narrator

The interface between the real and the fictional. 118 x 169 cm, oil on canvas, 1989-90, collection: Chester and Davida Herwitz, Worcester, USA

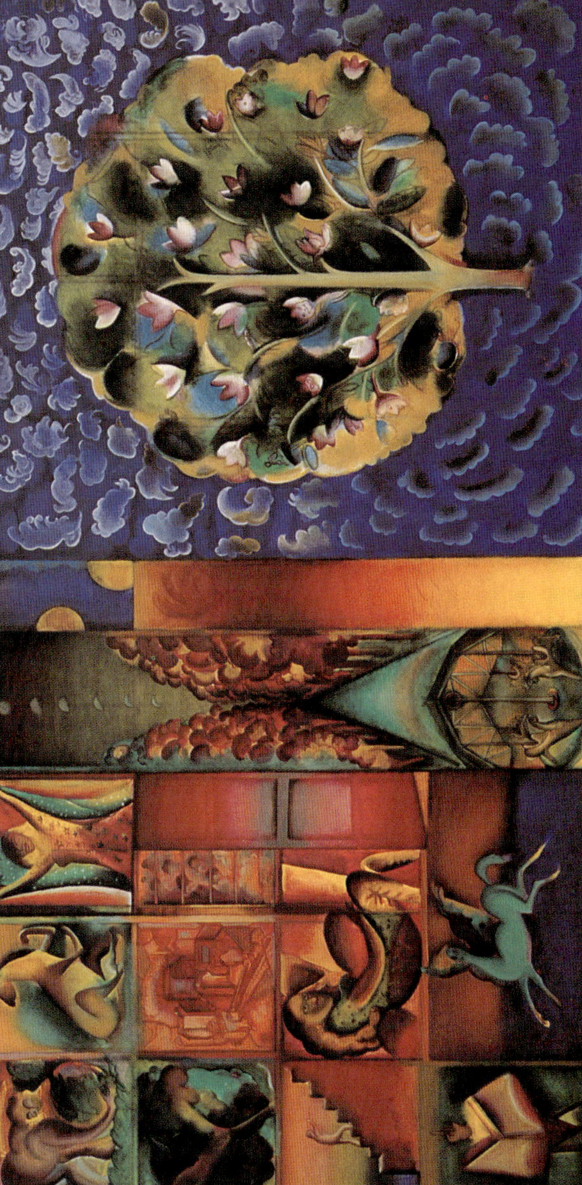

■ Memory and Music

One of a series of six panels painted for The Times of India office in New Delhi. 106.5 x 213.4 cm, oil on canvas, 1991, collection: The Times of India, New Delhi

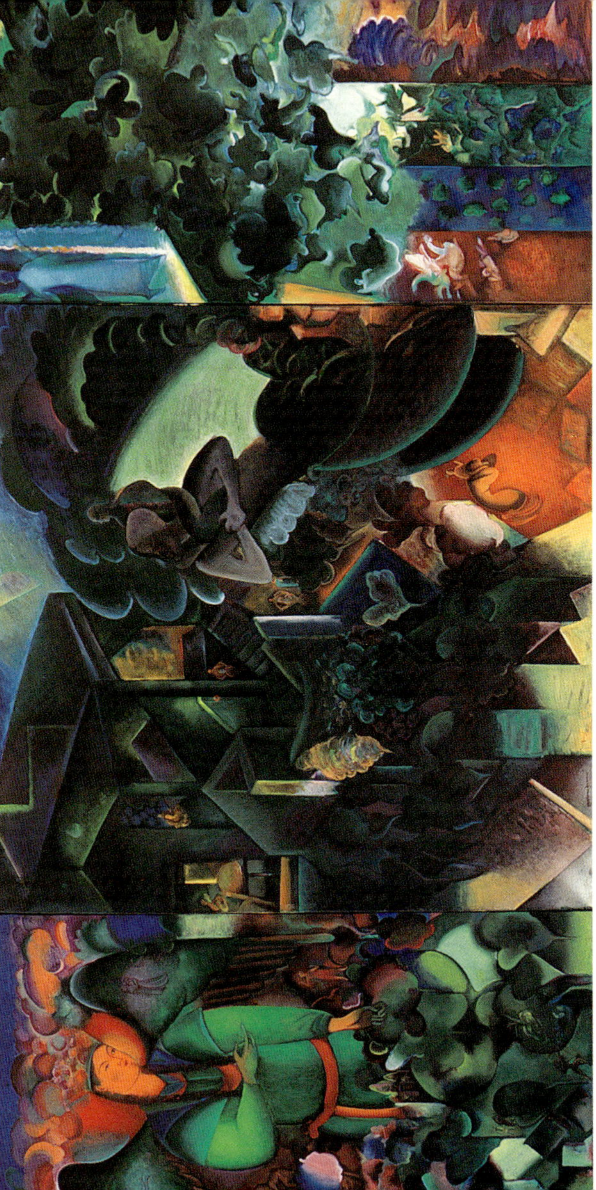

■ Visitation [triptych]

The angel in the left panel is 'quoted' from a Persian painting. 153 x 306 cm, oil on canvas, 1992-96, collection: Sahney, Mumbai

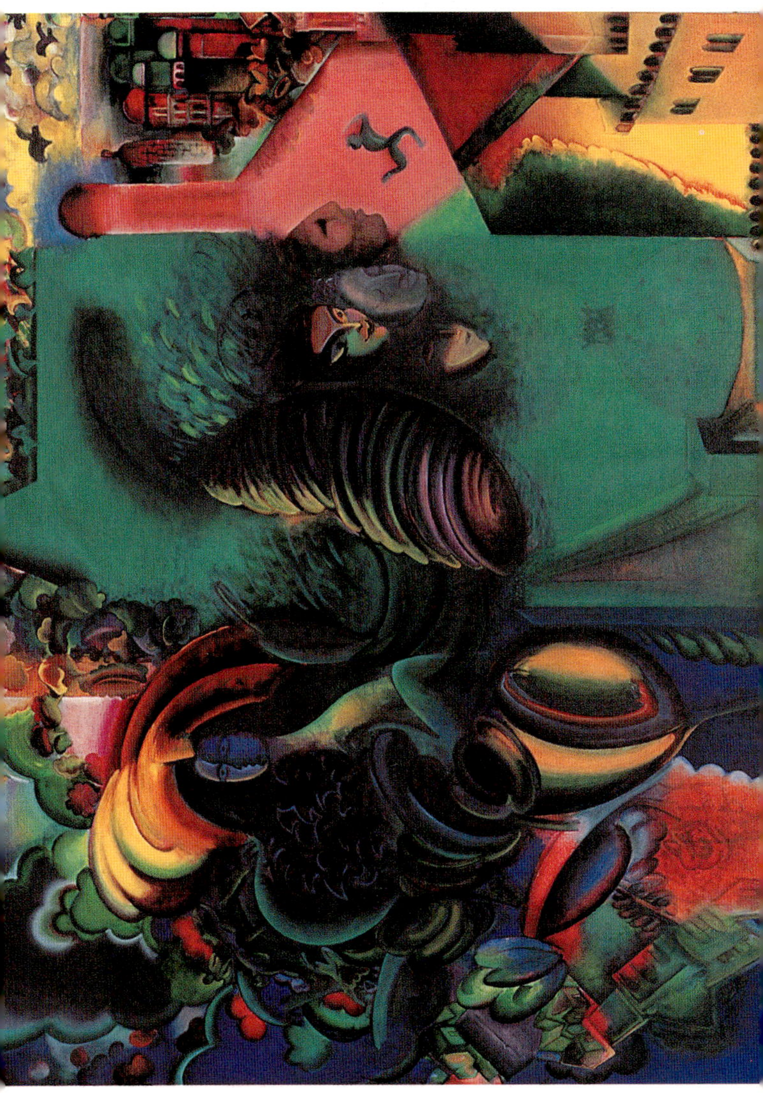

■ Choice of Birth

Where dreams mate with reality. 153.6 x 213.4 cm, oil on canvas, 1992-94, collection: Formerly Herwitz Collection: sold at Sotheby's to undisclosed collector

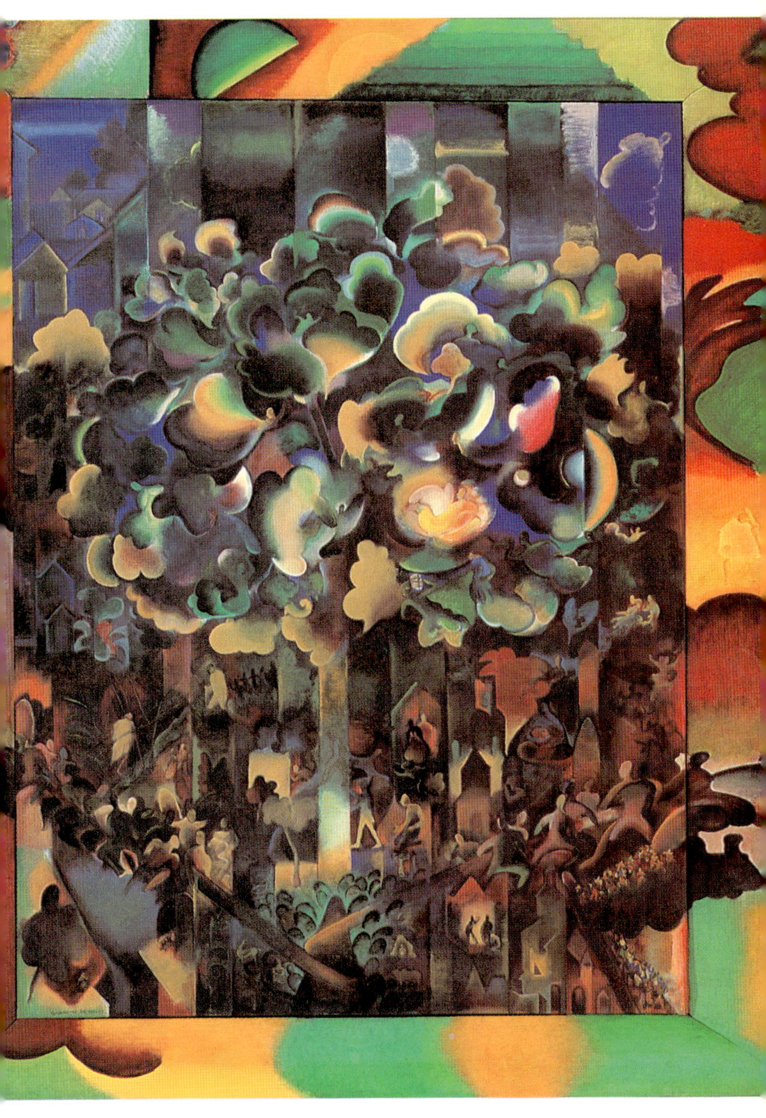

■ Freedom at Midnight/Speaking Tree II

Second in a series of exploratory paintings for the Vidhan Sabha mural in Bhopal. 200 x 159.5 cm, oil on canvas and wood, 1996, collection: Jindal Foundation, Mumbai

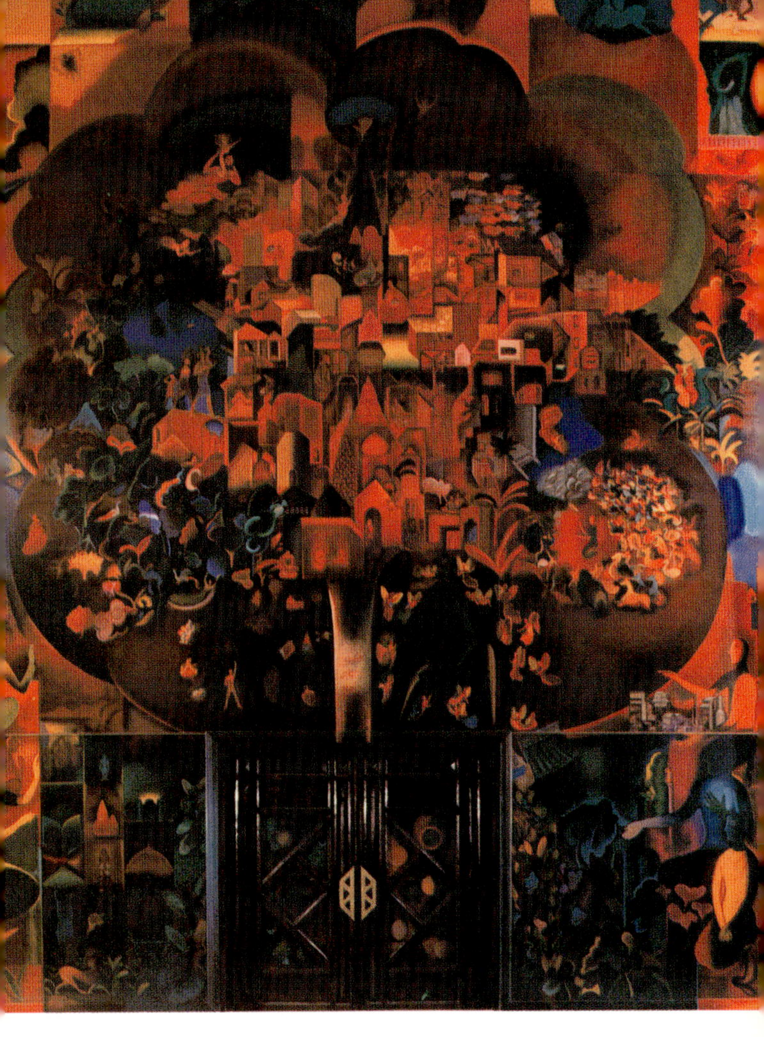

■ Tree of Life

Mural in thirteen panels on the entrance wall of the Legislative Assembly. 8.49 x 6.67 mtrs, oil on canvas mounted on plywood, 1996-97, installed at Vidhan Parishad entrance, Vidhan Bhavan, Bhopal

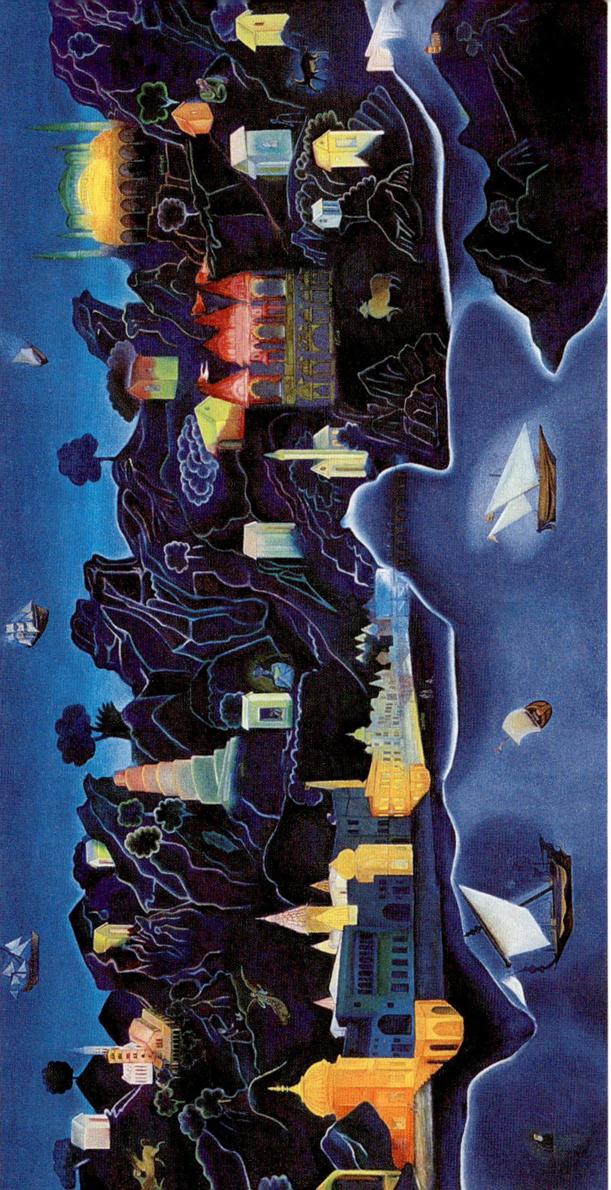

■ Numens [After the 'Thebaid' by Gherardo Starnina c. 1420]

A re-paint of Gherardo Starnina's Thebaid [c. 1420] with insertions of sacred sites of Ayodhya, Istanbul etc,
108.3 x 220 cm, oil on canvas wood, 2001, collection: Mrs and Mr Mishra, New Delhi

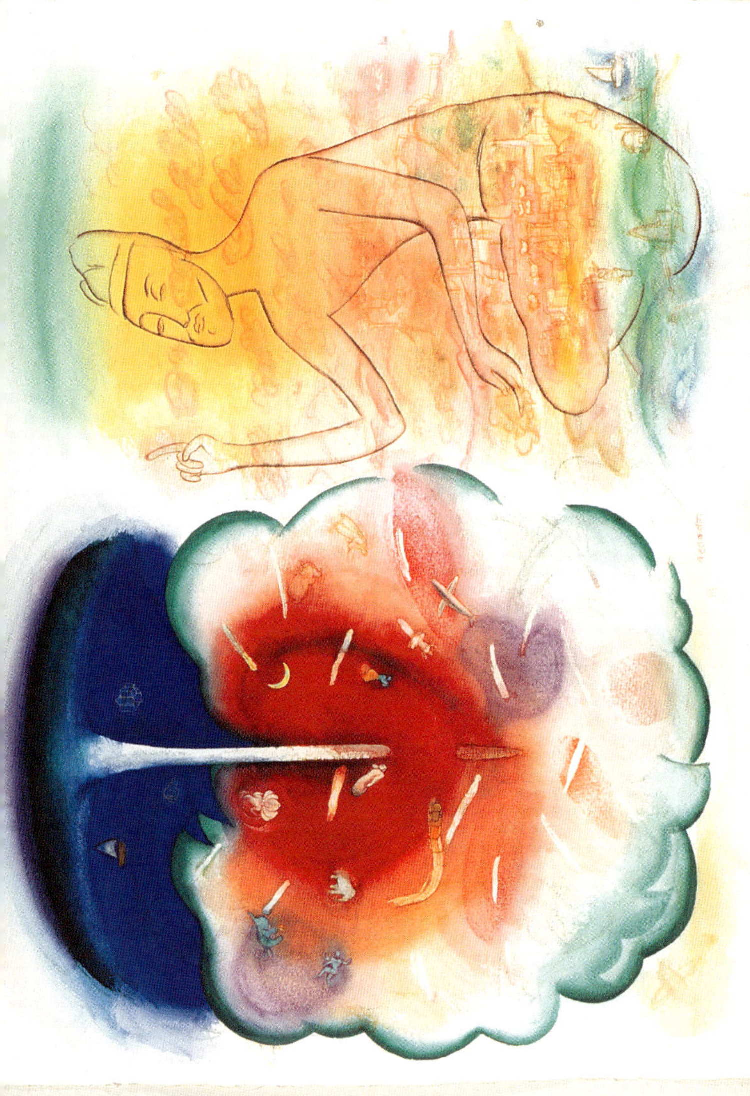

■ Kahat Kabir [Reversible]

Poet Kabir as a silent interlocutor on contemporary Indian life. 56 x76 cm, gouache, collection: Lalit Narula, New Delhi

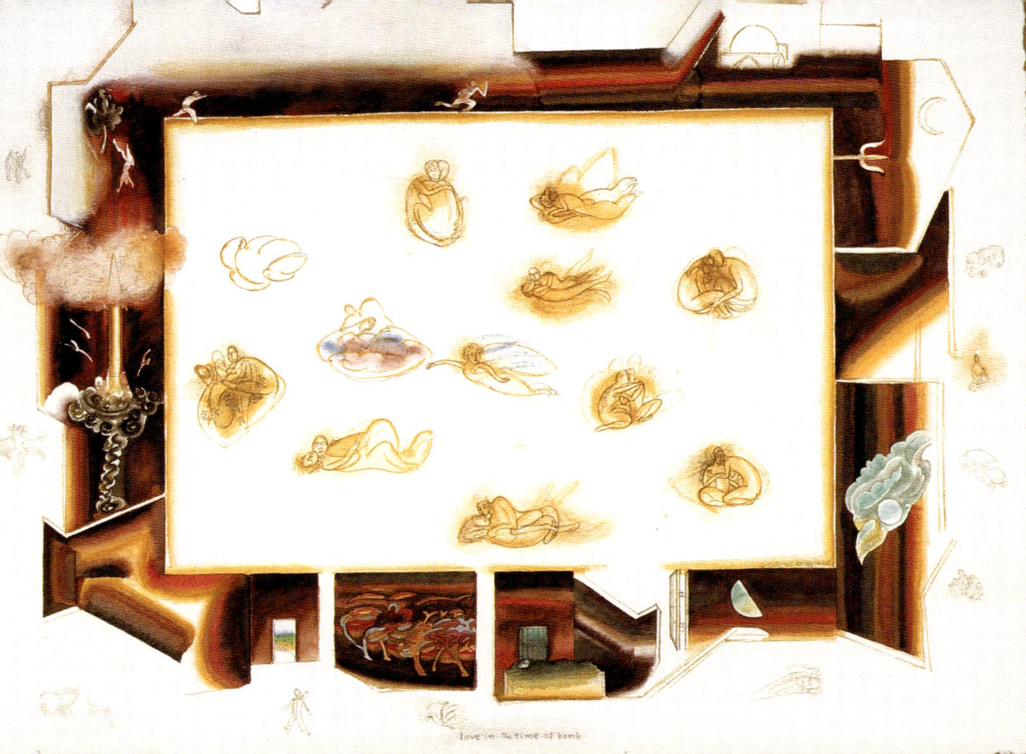
love in the time of bomb

■ Love in the Time of the Bomb

Juxtaposes the sensuous with the ominous in the aftermath of the nuclear test at Pokharan. 56 x 76 cm, gouache, 1998, collection: Lekha Poddar, New Delhi

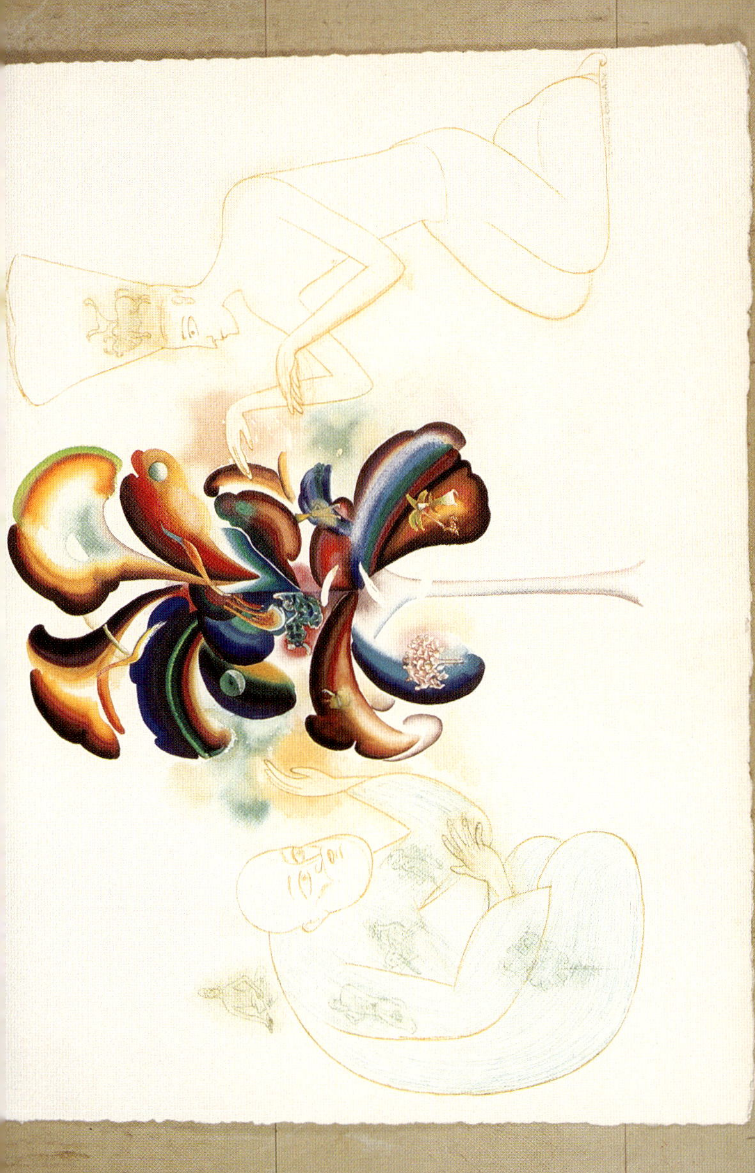

■ Conjurers

The irony of magic and creativity. 56 x 76 cm, gouache, 1998, collection: Praful Shah, Surat

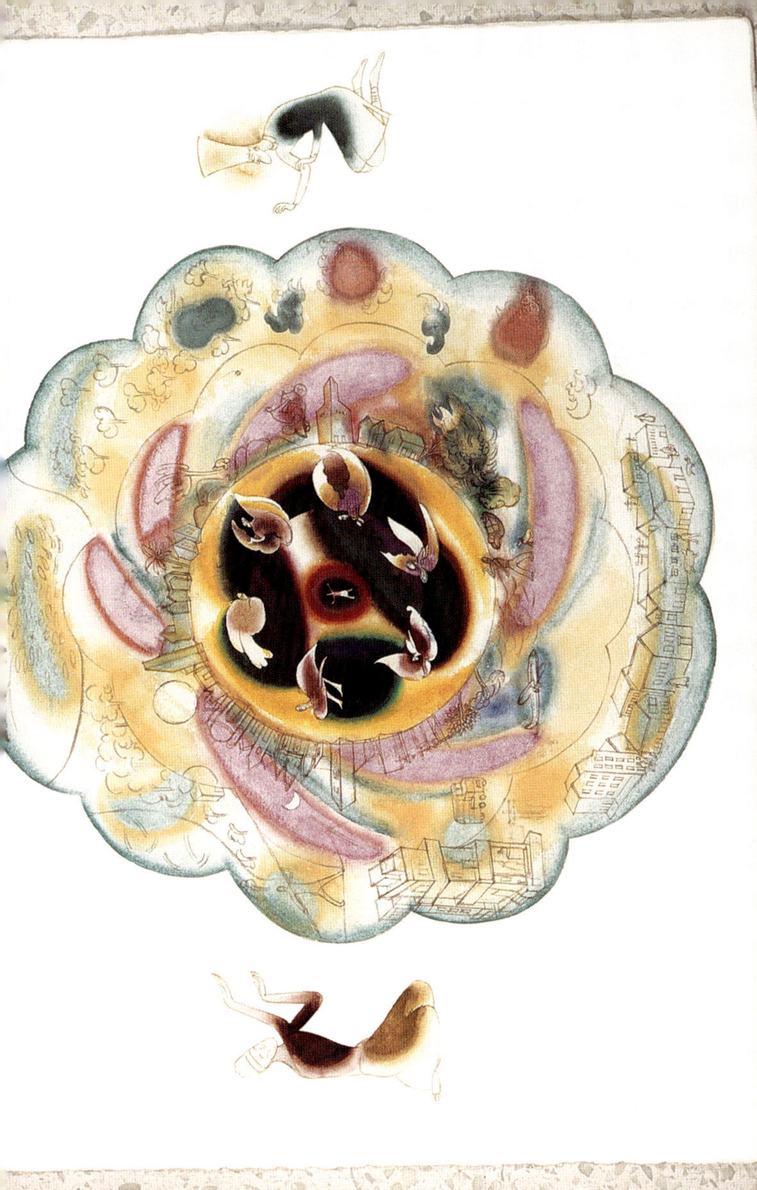

■ Poet and Magician

With Kabir as the central figure, the alchemy of poetry and the 'art' of magic are examined. 56 x 76 cm. gouache. 2000

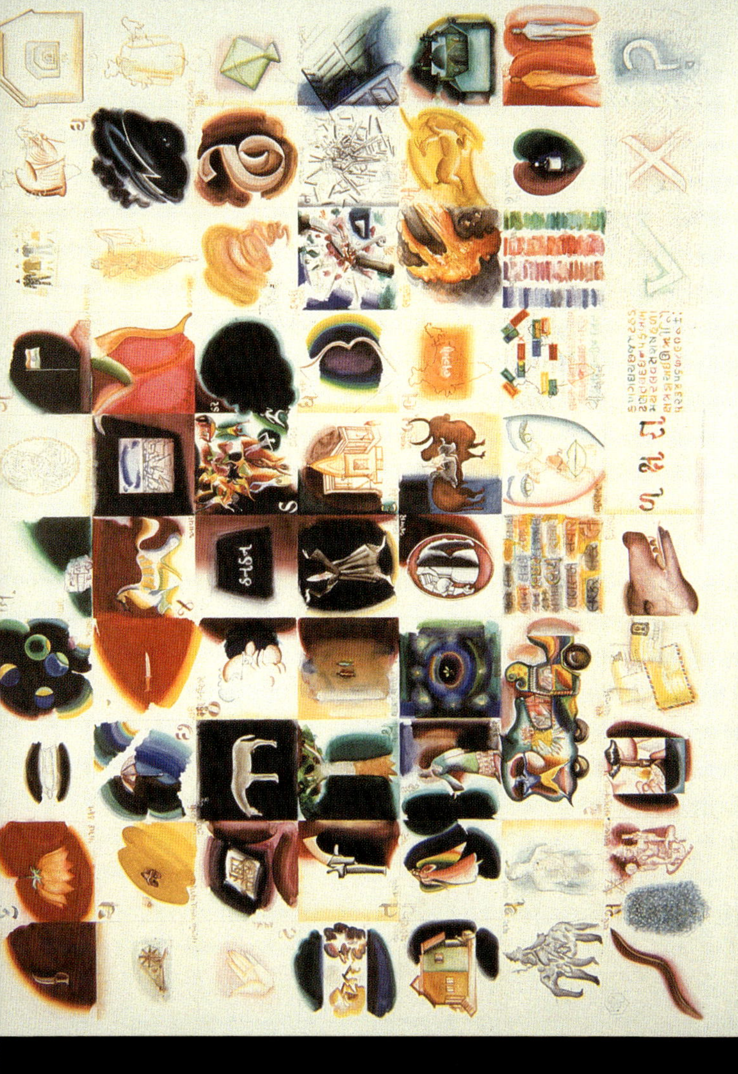

■ Alphabet Stories

A comment on the attempts at the rewriting of history. 180 x 210 cm, gouache, crayon, etc on paper, 2000, collection: B. Arunkumar, Mumbai

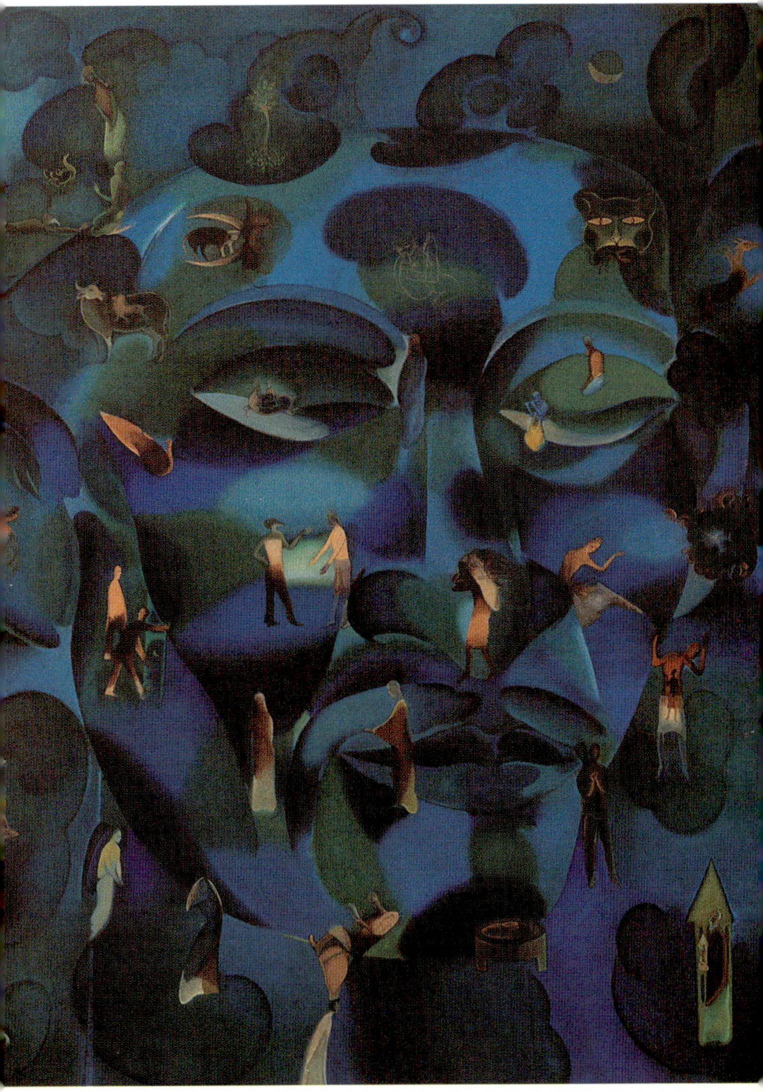

■ Kahat Kabir - Ek Achambha Dekha re Bhai

Using Kabir's verse, the painting explores the ironies of life.
213 x 167 cm, oil on canvas, 2001, collection: Jyoti Limited, Vadodara

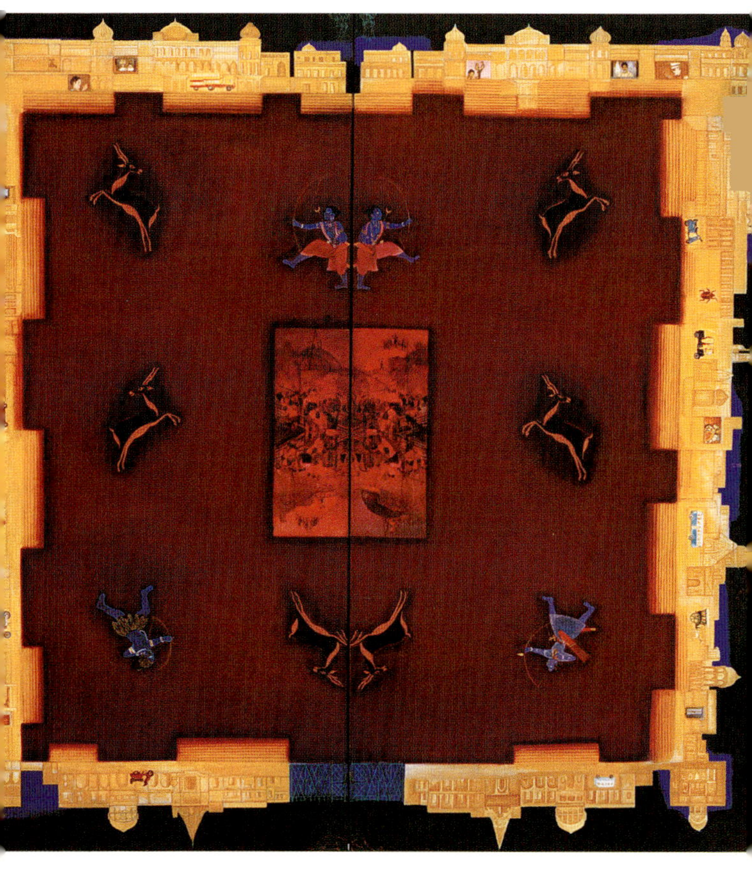

■ Mirage

The Ayodhya cityscape juxtaposes Rama's chase of the golden deer with the demolition of the Babri mosque.
213 x 212 cm, oil on canvas, 2001, collection: Ravi Sinha, London

■ *Front Cover:* The Story of Aziz and Aziza

This painting is based on a story from the Arabian Nights. 167.6 x 122 cm, oil on canvas, 1989, collection: Sahney, Mumbai

■ *Pages 2-3:* The painter in his world

Gulammohammed Sheikh, brush in hand, easel in front, epitomises the painter.